Path of Destruction

THE HISTORIC DEVASTATION AND RESTORATION OF DEKALB COUNTY

DEKALB COUNTY'S OLDEST NEWSPAPER

TIMES-JOURNAL

FOREWORD

CHALLENGES RARELY COME IN PIECES, and they almost never come quietly. Instead, they arrive collectively with force and fury. They bring with them fear, confusion and often an almost overwhelming sense of helplessness.

It all came April 27, 2011.

On a spring day that began with the rumble of thunder and a frightening tease of the mighty power Mother Nature planned to show off, an historic challenge came to DeKalb County, Alabama.

Unfortunately, this rural area has become accustomed to the force leveled by tornadoes. What had been a rare occurrence over the years suddenly had become almost typical. In the course of a year, six tornadoes touched the mountains and valleys DeKalb County families called home for generations. By the end of that day, the number would swell to 12.

When the wind stopped and the clouds finally raced away, the number did not matter. By late afternoon on April 27, only pain and loss and devastation were important. Never before had DeKalb County been ravaged in such a way. Never before had communities been destroyed with such violence. Never before had so many homes, so many businesses and so many lives been lost.

Never before had such a challenge been issued.

Amazingly, the story was the same all across central and north Alabama. From renowned cities like Tuscaloosa to tiny hamlets like Henagar, destruction reigned. One of the largest tornado outbreaks in Alabama history had left nearly 250 dead, thousands homeless and hundreds of thousands searching for any semblance of normalcy.

The most important characteristic of challenges, though, has little to do with the hardship. In fact, it's the opposite. Through challenge comes opportunity.

Through destruction comes rebuilding. Through loss comes love.

The memories of April 27, 2011 will not be of massive tornadoes that unleashed their wrath on a small county tucked in the foothills of the Appalachian Mountains. The hearts of the people who call this place home would never allow such pain to carry forward. What will live on for generations will be the fierce determination, unbridled love and the unique kinship forged as a community comes together.

That will be our story. That will be our legacy. That will be our future.

J.D. Davidson
Times-Journal President and Publisher

TABLE OF CONTENTS

CATASTROPHIC

Tragedy brings pride to mind

Editor's Note: This column originally appeared in the April 30-May 1, 2011 edition of the Times-Journal.

SITTING HERE, I DON'T KNOW what to say. Speechless. The more I hear the more words slip away. Speechless.

That's not right. No, that's not us. We speak. We shout. We roar. We live. That's what we do. That's what we always do. That's the only thing we can do. We wouldn't want it any other way.

Our pain is immeasurable, and it will last. These wounds will not be covered easily. Then, when the time comes, the scars will not be ignored.

But it will not be the hurt or those scars that will remind us of the day clouds roared and unleashed their power on our families, our friends, and our neighbors. It will not be our emptiness or our fear or our amazement that hold our attention to those minutes that stretch timelessly into days.

It couldn't be that. It wouldn't be those things. That is not us.

What will always be mentioned first is not the deadliest tornado in DeKalb County history. We will not talk of wind speeds or power scales or even the distance traveled. Those things will be gone quickly.

They don't have the muscle to hold us or the stamina to walk with us.

Instead, it will be the moments after. It will be the time when the sky cleared, our breath slowed, our minds focused and we became a family.

We did not look to see who was standing next to us. Nor did we shy away or slip into the background when a neighbor's cry shook us from our shock. We held hands, firmly. We lovingly held each other. At that moment, even though we didn't realize it, we began our journey forward. And, we did it together.

There are so many others who made our recovery part of their mission. They have come from everywhere, not knowing where they were headed or whom they were helping. They will always be remembered, and our thanks will never be enough. They are part of us, and certainly we will always be a part of them.

But the legacy left by this disaster will be carried by those who travel our roads, learn in our schools, visit our businesses and pray in our churches every day. That legacy will be rich. It will be strong. It will be astonishing.

What seems the most unsettling is there are no answers. No matter how much we wish, how hard we search and how forcefully we push, a reason for April 27, 2011 will never exist. It's in our nature, though, to keep looking.

Some will find comfort from the pursuit. Any comfort now, next week, next month or years from now will be welcome. Keep looking. Keep caring. Never give up.

I know exactly what to say. We will move forward. We will recover. We will do it shoulder-to-shoulder, hand-in-hand. The words fit perfectly into the most imperfect situation. In the dark, wondering where food might be, worrying about what tomorrow might bring, the word is pride.

In the wake of the storm, in the sorrow of those precious lives lost and in the midst of our rubble, I am proud to be part of this community. Those words come easily.

— J.D. Davidson
President and Publisher

OPPOSITE: Little remained of a home on Sylvania Gap Road as debris was scattered around. Three people survived the direct hit of an EF-5 tornado April 27.

Times-Journal photo by Melissa Smith

RIGHT: An EF-5 tornado that led a path of destruction ¾ mile wide and 34 miles long was photographed atop Lookout Mountain.

Photo by Jimmy Durham

OPPOSITE: Winds at 200 mph snapped power poles in half and left debris scattered for miles immediately after an EF-5 tornado ripped through a neighborhood in Rainsville.

Times-Journal photo by Melissa Smith

BELOW: Moments after a tornado dissected DeKalb County, a path of destruction was evident at Plainview School and other areas in Rainsville.

Times-Journal photo by Jared Felkins

ABOVE: A tornado left a home in ruins and a large truck on its side just off County Road 27 near Sylvania. The truck driver was inside when the tornado struck, but he walked away from the incident.

Times-Journal photo by Lonnie McKelvey

ABOVE: A brick house was partially destroyed on County Road 27 near Sylvania. The tornado packed 200-mph winds, but left many of the bricks in tact.

Times-Journal photo by Lonnie McKelvey

LEFT: Tornadoes removed the roof and many of the exterior walls from a home in the High Point community of DeKalb County, leaving the contents exposed and debris scattered throughout.

Times-Journal photo by Melissa Smith

OPPOSITE: Though a home was nearly completely destroyed in the High Point community near Ider, the residents' couch remained in its original spot.

Times-Journal photo by Melissa Smith

ABOVE: A tattered American flag flew above the remains of a home on Lingerfelt Road in Rainsville just days after an EF-5 tornado caused damage there.

Times-Journal photo by Lindsay Slater

RIGHT: Concrete lay scattered around a silo in the High Point community near Ider left by tornadoes that swept through April 27.

Times-Journal photo by Melissa Smith

ABOVE: Rainsville residents reel in the shock moments after an EF-5 tornado ripped through DeKalb County as DeKalb-Cherokee Gas District workers assessed damage.

Times-Journal photo by Jared Felkins

LEFT: A Rainsville resident walks among downed power lines in front of the DeKalb County Schools Coliseum moments after a tornado hit.

Times-Journal photo by Jared Felkins

FAR LEFT: An aerial view of Rainsville shows the path of destruction left by an EF-5 tornado with damaged homes and businesses and trees laid over on the ground.

Times-Journal photo by Melissa Smith

TOP: Teresa Spence walks among what is left of her home on Sylvania Gap Road near Sylvania after a tornado left it in near ruins.

Times-Journal photo by Melissa Smith

BOTTOM: Little more than the foundation remained at this Sylvania Gap Road home hit by 200 mph winds from an EF-5 tornado.

Times-Journal photo by Lonnie McKelvey

OPPOSITE: Nothing was left standing, including the family vehicle, at this home on County Road 27 after an EF-5 tornado struck.

Times-Journal photo by Melissa Smith

LEFT: It's difficult to distinguish debris from what's left of a home on Lingerfelt Road in Rainsville.

Times-Journal photo by Lindsay Slater

FAR LEFT: Little remained where two houses and Cherished Times Rentals used to stand on County Road 27 near Sylvania.

Times-Journal photo by Melissa Smith

BELOW: Debris was left scattered for miles in a path of destruction ¾ mile wide through the center of DeKalb County, hitting homes, businesses and a church on Sylvania Gap Road.

Times-Journal photo by Tammy Walker

RIGHT: The front page of the Times-Journal two days after six tornadoes ripped through DeKalb County featured the devastation and destruction, and one word described it all.

Times-Journal image

OPPOSITE TOP: A home in the High Point community near Ider was hit twice, first with its roof being blown off by a tornado and second with a large oak tree blown onto it.

Times-Journal photo by Melissa Smith

OPPOSITE BOTTOM LEFT & RIGHT: The powerful tornado that ripped through the High Point community picked up pavement and left it distributed in the grass on the right-of-way.

Times-Journal photo by Melissa Smith

CURRENT REPORTS AT WWW.TIMES-JOURNAL.COM

CURFEWS ESTBALISHED FOR DEKALB COUNTY AND MUNICIPALITIES

DEKALB COUNTY'S OLDEST NEWSPAPER

TIMES-JOURNAL

April 29, 2011

FRIDAY

Only 50 cents

CATASTROPHIC

Times-Journal photo by Jared Felkins

ON THE WEB
- Complete, up-to-date information regarding storm recovery, utility information, school information.
- Register for free to receive immediate breaking news alerts regarding

Dozens dead; many missing in DeKalb's deadliest storm

TVA: No

ABOVE: The power of an EF-5 tornado sent a piece of wood through the brick wall of the Best Western motel in Rainsville like a javelin.

Times-Journal photo by Melissa Smith

ABOVE: The contents of a home near Sylvania were distributed throughout the yard as little was left of the structure itself.

Times-Journal photo by Tammy Walker

LEFT: A large tree was uprooted by a tornado in the Town Creek church cemetery barely missing a headstone.

Times-Journal photo by Melissa Smith

ABOVE: The tornadoes' fury left Mountain View Baptist Church, homes and trees in a pile of rubble along County Road 27 near Sylvania.

Times-Journal photo by Tammy Walker

LEFT: DeKalb County saw significant damage to power lines, including this area near County Road 108 in Rainsville after tornadoes ripped through April 27.

Times-Journal photo by Lonnie McKelvey

OUR RECOVERY

April 27 was a nightmare for me and so many others

Editor's Note: This column originally appeared in the May 5, 2011 edition of the Times-Journal.

APRIL 27 IS A DAY that I will never forget. It could have been my last.

I've never given much thought to how I would die, but those thoughts raced through my mind as my co-worker, Mark Harrison, and I attempted to outrun an EF-5 tornado on County Road 27 in Sylvania.

The details are not as vivid in my mind now, and part of me is thankful that I can't recall everything that happened.

We got the call a tornado was on the ground in Fyffe, so I grabbed my camera and jumped in my car, thinking that I could get around the tornado and get some photos. I put the car in gear, and Mark opened the passenger door and said that he was coming with me.

We headed up Sylvania Gap, and we almost made it to the crossing when we saw what we thought was a wall cloud. I turn the car around, and then we could see it, and it was coming straight for us.

In a panic, I pulled into the driveway of a brick house, thinking maybe we could pound on the door and get inside, but by that time, the tornado was close, so close I could feel it picking up my car. I turned around, and sped toward Rainsville as fast as my little car would go.

All I could think about was the fact I was responsible for us because I was driving, and I wrecked my car in the process. After the wreck, my car miraculously kept running, and we headed to Rainsville for safety.

We did get out alive, and I couldn't be more thankful. I laid in my bed that night, unable to sleep. I can't remember the last time I had prayed so hard, and thanked God for sparing my life.

Friday, I went back to the brick house on County Road 27. I walked up the driveway and introduced myself to the owner.

"You're the girl in the white car, aren't you?" he exclaimed, with wide eyes. "I saw you pull in the driveway and I came to the back door to let you in, but then the tornado came.

I stood there, with tears in my eyes and he hugged me.

"Young 'en, I've been looking for you and your car since Wednesday night, I just knew you didn't make it. I just knew you didn't."

It took a little while for those words to sink in, and all I could do was stand there and cry.

It's difficult to put this situation into words, but it's just a nightmare. It's an absolute nightmare.

To everyone that has lost everything, including loved ones, I am truly sorry.

— Melissa Smith
Chief Photographer

OPPOSITE: In the path of an EF-5 tornado, this picture was taken just moments before the photographer and another staff writer found themselves outrunning the twister.

Times-Journal photo by Melissa Smith

ABOVE: Debris from homes on Sylvania Gap Road were caught among the branches of the few trees that remained.

Times-Journal photo by Lonnie McKelvey

TOP RIGHT: Areas in Rainsville and other parts of DeKalb County resembled more of a war zone than a rural Alabama community after tornadoes struck on April 27.

Times-Journal photo by Lindsay Slater

RIGHT: A billboard advertising nearby Zaxby's in Fort Payne was brought to the ground in Rainsville by an EF-5 tornado April 27.

Times-Journal photo by Mandi Cooper

ABOVE: Chickens are scattered in the Shiloh community after a chicken house was destroyed by a tornado.

Times-Journal photo by Mandi Cooper

LEFT: The sign at Grace Chapel Baptist Church at Town Creek in Rainsville was removed from its brick enclosure.

Times-Journal photo by Lindsay Slater

FAR LEFT: A large portion of Grace Chapel Baptist Church at Town Creek was removed by a tornado April 27, leaving the church in near ruins.

Times-Journal photo by Lindsay Slater

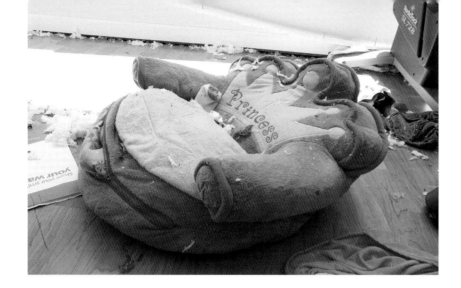

ABOVE: Residents work to collect the remains of what was left of a home on County Road 27 from an EF-5 tornado.

Times-Journal photo by Melissa Smith

TOP LEFT: Remnants of homes in the path of destruction, including this child's chair in a home on County Road 27, were a reminder of the destruction from April 27.

Times-Journal photo by Melissa Smith

LEFT: An 'X' was spray painted on a home on Lingerfelt Road in Rainsville to signify all clear following a search after it was significantly damaged by a tornado.

Times-Journal photo by Lindsay Slater

OPPOSITE: Grace Chapel Baptist Church at Town Creek in Rainsville suffered significant damage from an EF-5 tornado April 27.

Times-Journal photo by Lindsay Slater

OUR RECOVERY

A View From Inside

Editor's Note: This story originally appeared in the May 7-8, 2011 edition of the Times-Journal.

MANY PEOPLE GOT A GOOD look at the tornado that decimated DeKalb County on April 27, but one Henagar resident got a unique – and frightening – view from inside the twister.

Kathy Crow McBride, 28, of Henagar, was inside a pickup truck which got tossed by the tornado. She said her ordeal began after some friends of hers from Flat Rock called her up and asked if she had a cellar at her home on County Road 138.

At first, she thought it was a joke. It wasn't. Her friends were actually seeking shelter from what would turn out to be one of the worst storm systems in history. As it turned out, McBride did have a cellar, and she and her friends spent a good portion of Wednesday inside of it, until one friend got a call that the storm had caused damage to his home in Flat Rock.

McBride said she and her friends took off to check out the damage and, when they got there, found that his home had been demolished – but the worst of the storm wasn't over yet. It was late Wednesday afternoon and they soon heard of another, even stronger storm headed their way from Rainsville.

The trio loaded back up and tried to make it back to McBride's cellar to again seek shelter, traveling in a full-size Chevrolet pickup.

They never made it back to the cellar.

As they traveled along County Road 117, McBride said she spotted the tornado – the very tornado the

National Weather Service would later classify as an EF-5, the most powerful known – three quarters of a mile wide, with wind speeds of 200 mph. And there was nowhere to go.

"Someone kept yelling 'gun it, gun it,' but I knew that it didn't matter how fast we were going, we weren't going to make it," McBride said. "It was huge. A monster. There was just nowhere to go."

She said her friend who was driving, in a desperate attempt to stay alive, plunged the nose of the truck into a nearby ditch and the three clung together as the tornado overtook them. She said it picked up the back of the heavy truck and flung it around as it passed over, but fortunately deposited the truck more completely into the ditch instead of lifting it out.

McBride and her friends then experienced

something few have likely ever lived to tell about, the experience of being inside a tornado.

"It was just swirling blackness," she said. "Darkness – it was just dark. And the pressure started building up in the cab of the truck – I thought my eardrums were going to explode."

They didn't, but a windshield did, blowing in from the pressure and the truck was also pelted with debris, including a nearby stop sign the twister picked up and slammed into the truck. McBride said she did the only thing she could think to do.

"I grabbed my friends, and I started praying," she said. "It's the scariest thing I have ever been through in my life. It lasted maybe less than a minute, but it felt like forever."

She said, once the storm passed and she realized that she and her friends were alright, she realized they were near her cousin's house, close to the intersection of 117 and 138.

"Once I realized that, my first thought was that we

ABOVE: The tornadoes' fury was evident near Ider with the contents of this home scattered all around, as well as the absence of several trees.

Times-Journal photo by Melissa Smith

OPPOSITE: A truck in the parking lot of Katy's Katfish in Rainsville has the tell-tale signs it went through a tornado with dirt and grass caked on its dashboard.

Times-Journal photo by Melissa Smith

could go there but then I looked up in that direction and I suddenly realized that their house was gone," she said. "It was just gone."

It seemed McBride's horrifying ordeal would never end. She managed to get out of the truck and run to the remnants of her cousin's home.

"I wasn't even thinking about myself at that point," she said. "I was worried about them. Then I realized that it wasn't just their home, but all the houses around had been destroyed, too. People started climbing out of the rubble and someone told me that my cousins weren't home."

She tried to call her cousins, to call someone – but she couldn't – her cell phone wouldn't work. Nothing

would. "We live in an age of technology and you get used to having all of those sort of things and then it's just gone, and you're surrounded by all this destruction and there's just nothing. I'm standing there and there are homes that had been there my whole life that are gone and you think that, in the face of something like that, there's nothing you can do – you just feel completely helpless."

McBride – a clerk at Ider Drugs – soon found herself telling her story to patrons of the business. She returned to work after her experience to help others in need, doling out medication to those in Ider even while the business remained without power. If the experience had shaken her, it was difficult to tell,

as she calmly helped hand out prescriptions.

"I'm just thankful to be alive, that my family is alive and that my friends are alive," she said. "I do know that's something I don't ever want to experience again."

— Mark Harrison,
Staff Writer

ABOVE: The roof of a home, along with several surrounding trees, were tossed around by a tornado in the High Point community near Ider.

Times-Journal photo by Melissa Smith

LEFT: Brick columns and walls lay on the ground exposing the inside of a home destroyed by the most destructive storm in DeKalb County's history.

Times-Journal photo by Melissa Smith

OPPOSITE LEFT: Debris littered the Plainview School campus just days after an EF-5 tornado caused significant damage to the school April 27.

Times-Journal photo by Melissa Smith

OPPOSITE RIGHT: A storm shelter remained in tact with debris scattered all around in the High Point community near Ider.

Times-Journal photo by Melissa Smith

I feel sorry about what the tornado did. I bet it is hard living and sleeping in shelters. I watched the news this morning and heard people ███████ that survived the tornado. I feel very sad. ☹ 8   My name is   I am from   Riley   Auburn Al

If your house gets redill I hope you are safe.

ABOVE: A truckload of supplies arrived from Auburn along with a drawing and note from 8-year-old Riley Jackson that brought about a flurry of emotions among DeKalb volunteers.

Times-Journal photo by Mark Harrison

RIGHT: A Sylvania girl tries to recover precious items among a sea of rubble at her home on County Road 27.

Times-Journal photo by Melissa Smith

OPPOSITE: Alabama Gov. Robert Bentley made a surprise visit to services May 1 at Mountain View Baptist Church after an EF-5 tornado destroyed the church.

Photo by Mary Felkins

Times-Journal

DEKALB COUNTY'S OLDEST NEWSPAPER

WEEKEND

April 30-May 1, 2011

Only 75 cents

MEDICAL ISSUES ONGOING
EMERGENCY HEALTH CARE ESTABLISHED - INSIDE, PAGE 6
ALSO: FEMA SETTING UP MOBILE RELIEF CENTERS IN RAINSVILLE, PAGE 6

OUR RECOVERY

DeKalb tornado rated one of the strongest on scale

PRESIDENT OBAMA TOURS DESTRUCTION IN TUSCALOOSA ■ PAGE 4

Times-Journal photo by Melissa Smith

Carol Haney stands in the bathtub where she and her husband and son took shelter during the tornado that ripped through DeKalb County on Wednesday night.

INSIDE
■ RECOVERY SHIFT
■ TRASH PICK-UP
■ OBAMA DECLARES
■ GAS PRICES RISE

Classified 8
Dear Abby 11
Engagement 7

Forecaster may declare larger rating

By Jared Felkins
jfelkins@times-journal.com

"It was considered a violent tornado," said

J.D. DAVIDSON
*President
& Publisher
The Times-Journal*
jdavidson@times-journal.com

Tragedy brings pride

ABOVE: Teresa Spence's home on Sylvania Gap Road was completely destroyed except for one wall with a memorable quote stenciled on it. *Times-Journal photo by Melissa Smith*

LEFT: The Times-Journal's weekend edition following April 27 tornadoes remained focused on relief and recovery efforts across DeKalb County. *Times-Journal image*

OPPOSITE: As with hundreds of homes on Sand Mountain, this house in Ider was completely destroyed by a twister on April 27. *Times-Journal photo by Melissa Smith*

ABOVE: The outer walls and doors of a home in Section were removed by an early morning tornado that struck Jackson County and moved through on April 27.

Times-Journal photo by Melissa Smith

LEFT: An early-morning tornado that hit Section on April 27 left power lines downed and several homes without electricity.

Times-Journal photo by Melissa Smith

OPPOSITE: Members of the Ider Rescue Squad worked around the clock to provide tornado victims with supplies.

Times-Journal photo by Melissa Smith

OUR RESPONSE

Storm Survivor[3]

Editor's Note: This story originally appeared in the May 7-8, 2011 edition of the Times-Journal.

ED WITT LIKES TO FILL his home with music.

Fort Payne High School's track and field and cross country coach since 2005, Witt had five guitars and more than 1,600 CDs in his home on County Road 441 in Rainsville, near the Sylvania line.

Music is Witt's hobby; it was nearly his profession.

"Rather than finish college, I almost went on the road," he said.

Instead, he became a teacher and coach. In his early years as an educator — he started his career in 1968 — he would perform on Friday and Saturday nights. Rock, big band, country, blue grass, jazz. It was a way for Witt to recharge.

Over the years, Witt, 67, coached at Virginia, James Madison, Alabama and Wallace State. And wherever he went, his love of music went with him.

For Witt, April 27 could have been the day the music died.

That afternoon, a tornado ransacked most of his neighborhood. Witt, on his hands and knees in a bathtub, was almost buried alive as his house literally fell in around him, and that was only Part 1 of his ordeal.

Somehow, he survived, walking away with only a few bruises and cuts. A miracle almost too difficult to believe.

NEAR MISSES

The Weather Channel's Jim Cantore has nothing on Witt.

It's been said when Cantore comes to town, the best course is to leave because Mother Nature's fury is sure to follow.

Witt has seen his own share of natural disasters. In 1969, Witt was a second-year coach at Nelson County High School in Lovingston, Va., when Hurricane Camille dropped 38 inches of rain on the area in three hours.

Witt's home escaped damage, but many around him weren't as lucky. In a county of 14,000, the death toll was 275.

"It was lightning so much it never got dark," Witt remembered. "It camped out right over us.

[Afterwards], the power lines for miles and miles didn't exist. They just had to go back and rebuild the electrical system."

A few years ago, Witt just missed driving into a tornado near Nashville, Tenn.

Traffic came to a standstill during a period of extremely hard rain. When the rain ended, Witt pulled off to the side see why traffic hadn't started moving. When he looked up ahead, he saw trees down and cars flipped. Eventually, the path of the tornado became evident.

"Probably another five seconds of travel and I would have been right in the thick of it," Witt said. "That one took me totally by surprise. I had no clue I was so close to it."

Flash forward a few years, and Witt would find himself in the middle of a deadly twister.

IN THE EYE OF THE STORM

When the power went out on the afternoon of April 27, Witt sat down to play some guitar. About 45 minutes later, things began to go terribly wrong.

"I looked out the back door and thought, 'What a

OPPOSITE: Fort Payne High School track coach Ed Witt stands with his guitar that made it through a tornado inside his home that didn't.

Times-Journal photo by Lew Gilliland

black cloud,'" he said. "I started to go check it out. At that point. I started hearing that train sound. It was at a distance, but I could still hear that sound.

"I ran as fast as I could down the hall. I had a bathroom in the middle of the house. The first sign that I was in trouble was when I tried to shut the door and it wouldn't shut because the pressure was changing. I grabbed it and slammed it shut.

"I don't know what I did with the guitar. I just dove in the tub. I had my back toward the hall wall, toward the center of the house. I put my hands in front, shoulder width, and was on my knees. I prayed, 'Please help me through this.'

"I wasn't in the tub more than three seconds before the house started shaking."

Witt felt the inner walls and ceiling collapsing on and around him as he tried to brace himself, fighting not to be buried in the rubble.

"I knew that I was going to be trapped," he said. "My lifetime in sports and the tenacity that goes with it and being able to react literally had saved my life to that point because there is no time to think. Everything from there was a miracle."

GOING AIRBORNE

Just when Witt felt he couldn't hold up any longer, things changed.

"The roof just went," he said. "I don't know where it went, it just went up. As soon as the roof left … everything that was on me just started to lighten up. When everything went, the wall in front of me went, too."

But Witt's ordeal wasn't over. The twister also picked up the bathroom floor and bathtub — with Witt in it. Eventually, Witt and the tub became separated.

"I could literally see the floor beneath me start to fly," he said. "For the life of me, I don't have a single memory of when I left the bath tub."

Witt said he never blacked out during the entire ordeal, which he estimates lasted 15 seconds. He landed about 75 yards from his home, in one of the few spaces not covered by debris.

"It didn't hurt, and all I know is I landed with my back toward where the tornado was going, which was away from me, and I just laid there because I did not want to look at it," he said.

"It happened so fast and so many things are going through your mind, I don't think fear is a factor. It's like how do you survive."

THE AFTERMATH

Eric Roberts was the friend Witt called for help in the aftermath of the storm. Witt took off running and met Roberts about 2 miles up the road. It was the next day, when they returned to the scene, the Roberts saw the destruction in Witt's neighborhood for the first time.

"My first thought was he's blessed to be alive," Roberts said. "I don't believe in luck. I think he's blessed.

"I remember the '74 tornado and remember a church being destroyed, but never this big a path [of destruction]."

For his part, Witt believes there's a reason his life was spared.

"A cousin said to me, 'God has something left for you to do,'" Witt said. "And I said, 'I know there is, but I don't know what it is. I think I'll recognize it when it comes along, and I am going to be there.'"

RIGHT ALONG WITH HIS MUSIC

The five guitars in Witt's house when the tornado hit all survived, including the one he was playing, the one he couldn't remember dropping as he dove into the tub. When Witt pulled himself up after being sat down by the storm, that guitar was next to him, almost untouched.

"It's just as good as it ever was," he said, "just like me."

— Lew Gilliland
Sports Editor

ABOVE: A woman looks at the devastation in Rainsville left by a twister that ravaged several areas in DeKalb County.

Times-Journal photo by Lindsay Slater

LEFT: A woman and child walk around the destruction left by an EF-5 tornado that ripped through Rainsville.

Times-Journal photo by Lindsay Slater

OPPOSITE: A cross was built amid the rubble of a home on Lingerfelt Road in Rainsville.

Times-Journal photo by Lindsay Slater

ABOVE: The outer walls of the DeKalb County Schools Coliseum were blown off to reveal the inner bleachers and court floor by an EF-5 tornado on April 27.

Times-Journal photo by Melissa Smith

ABOVE: Precious mementos, such as this recipe book, could be found in the High Point community in the days following April 27 tornadoes.

Times-Journal photo by Melissa Smith

RIGHT TOP: Though an EF-5 tornado left a path ¾ miles wide through County Road 27 near Sylvania, some homes like this one were only partially damaged.

Times-Journal photo by Melissa Smith

RIGHT BOTTOM: Debris littered what was left of trees along the tornado-torn area on County Road 27 near Sylvania.

Times-Journal photo by Melissa Smith

RIGHT: Volunteers with Carpenters for Christ help rebuild Mountain View Church in Sylvania.

Times-Journal photo by Melissa Smith

BELOW: An emotional moment was shared on the National Day of Prayer at the DeKalb County Sheriff's Disaster Relief Center in Rainsville.

Times-Journal photo by Melissa Smith

ABOVE: After several instances of thefts among debris along County Road 27, signs started to emerge from tornado victims protecting what was left of their homes.

Times-Journal photo by Melissa Smith

ABOVE: This truck in Rainsville was among the many casualties of the April 27 tornadoes that devastated DeKalb County.

Times-Journal photo by Lindsay Slater

TOP: This storage shed was destroyed at a residence in Rainsville.

Times-Journal photo by Melissa Smith

BOTTOM: Williams Service Station in the High Point community served as a haven for tornado victims to get items they needed following the April 27 tornadoes.

Times-Journal photo by Melissa Smith

LEFT: Images like this one were numerous across Sand Mountain as debris was left scattered by devastating tornadoes.

Times-Journal photo by Lindsay Slater

OPPOSITE: Trees were uprooted, debris lay scattered but this home in the High Point community near Ider remained damaged but standing.

Times-Journal photo by Melissa Smith

BELOW: A home in the High Point community near Ider was basically dissected by powerful tornadoes that ripped through DeKalb on April 27.

Times-Journal photo by Melissa Smith

TOP: The Hester home was nearly destroyed by a tornado in the High Point community near Ider.

Times-Journal photo by Melissa Smith.

BOTTOM: The shell of a Rainsville brick home decimated by a tornado was left without a roof.

Times-Journal photo by Lindsay Slater

OPPOSITE: Workers try to clear debris in the High Point community near Ider. In all, six tornadoes struck DeKalb County on April 27.

Times-Journal photo by Melissa Smith.

TIMES-JOURNAL

DEKALB COUNTY'S OLDEST NEWSPAPER

—TUESDAY—

May 3, 2011

Only 50 cents

GOVERNOR PRAYS FOR DEKALB

BENTLEY TAKES PULPIT AT MOUNTAIN VIEW BAPTIST CHURCH, PAGE 10

OUR RESPONSE

■ Not one, but two tornadoes strike DeKalb County

FORT PAYNE SCHOOLS UNDECIDED ON HOW TO MAKE UP DAYS LOST ■ PAGE 9

Times-Journal photo by Melissa Smith

An emotional scene came at the remnants of Pine Grove Methodist Church, where services were held Sunday. The church was destroyed by one of the tornadoes that struck DeKalb County on Wednesday.

NWS: EF-4s hit within two hours

By Jared Felkins
jfelkins@times-journal.com

Two EF-4 tornadoes struck DeKalb County on April 27 within about two hours of one another, according to National Weather Service surveys.

A survey from the first tornado was completed and released Sunday night. According to NWS reports, the tornado touched down at 4:01 p.m. about 3 miles northeast of Section. It continued gaining intensity as it moved northeast through parts of Pisgah and Rosalie. According to the survey, residents said it was a multi-vortex tornado with up to

■ See Tornado, 3

Photo by Lindsay Slater

Congressman Robert Aderholt toured DeKalb County again Monday following last week's deadly tornado that struck Sand Mountain.

Aderholt promises help

By Lindsay Slater
lslater@times-journal.com

Congressman Robert Aderholt, along with FEMA and state EMA officials, returned to DeKalb County on Monday, again touring the devastation left by an EF-4 tornado that ripped through the area April 27.

"We are making sure resources are

■ See Aderholt, 3

MORE COVERAGE

Lessons: Galveston offers thoughts from its own tragedy involving Hurricane Ike .

Page 4

PHOTO GALLERIES
Get a complete visual timeline of DeKalb's response

FORECAST
HIGH 66 Low 36
Today will be rainy with showers through the day.

■ Page 2

To subscribe, call (256) 845-2550 or 1-800-34TIMES

LEFT: Volunteers, such as Barbara Hope and Liz Coots, served meals to tornado victims at Broadway Baptist Church in Rainsville.

Times-Journal photo by Lindsay Slater

OPPOSITE LEFT: The Times-Journal continued its coverage of devastating tornadoes that ripped through DeKalb County nearly a week prior.

Times-Journal image

OPPOSITE RIGHT: A large amount of items, including massive amounts of clothing, were donated to the Sheriff's Department Relief Center.

Times-Journal photo by Melissa Smith

BELOW: Supplies started pouring into DeKalb County from across the nation, including this tractor trailer load of items from Auburn.

Times-Journal photo by Mark Harrison

ABOVE: Devastation can be seen along both sides of Lingerfelt Road in Rainsville after an EF-5 tornado left a path ¾ miles wide.

Times-Journal photo by Lindsay Slater

RIGHT: Little remained but the concrete pads of where a mobile home park used to be in path of a destructive tornado that ripped through DeKalb County.

Times-Journal photo by Melissa Smith

OUR RESOLVE

The time came to cry

Editor's Note: This column originally appeared in the May 3, 2011 edition of the Times-Journal.

FOUR DAYS LATER, I CRIED.

Sitting among friends at church, I cried.

As the names of those who lost their lives from the furious force of last week's tornado were read aloud, I cried.

Listening to hymns of praise and power, I cried.

Watching others as they gently wiped away tears and tried to hold their emotions, I cried.

Thinking of those around me who had given so much to help those left in ruin, I cried.

Watching as so many fought to do so much more for so many, I cried

Feeling helpless and overwhelmed, I cried.

Wondering, worrying and trying to find answers, I cried.

Seeing picture after picture after picture of devastation and destruction, I cried.

Praying, I cried.

It was time. There has to be that time. No person, no neighborhood, no city, no county and no state can withstand the forces of destruction and the power of loss we have been assaulted with and not cry.

At some point, when the moment is right, we should cry. We cannot begin to heal without it. Until the unsettledness, the mourning, the anguish and the confusion comes flowing out and rolls down our battered cheeks, we cannot brush ourselves off completely.

Each day, for many, is better than the last. Better, though, is not always good. In fact, better for our community remains so far away from survivable, many continue to feel amazing despair. Better is a step on the rocky path toward progress, but to many one step leaves us asking how many more must be traveled on weary legs.

For them, I cry.

Then, I smiled.

Knowing the heart that lives within each of us in DeKalb County, I smiled.

Seeing the incredible will of those who lost everything picking up the pieces, I smiled.

Hearing story after story of church after church erecting a pulpit in the midst of rubble, I smiled.

Learning more and more of the true acts of heroism from firefighters, ambulance workers, paramedics, deputies, police officers, doctors and nurses, I smiled.

Thinking of the back-breaking work utility workers put themselves through to help bring back our lives, I smiled.

Watching as the Red Cross, churches and countless other organizations never asked if they were needed but ran into the disaster with arms widely spread, I smiled.

Seeing hundreds and hundreds of people from thousands of miles away here for our benefit, I smiled.

That's why those tears are needed. It's because they will turn to smiles. The people of DeKalb County will see that it does.

— J.D. Davidson
President and Publisher

OPPOSITE: Sunday morning services continued at Pine Grove Methodist Church in the High Point community just days after April 27. The pulpit was recovered and set up on the front steps.

Times-Journal photo by Melissa Smith

ABOVE: DeRinda Blevins walks in the ruins of what was once her home on Marshall Road in Rainsville.

Times-Journal photo by Lindsay Slater

LEFT: Only piles of and rubble were left after a tornado swept through Sand Mountain on April 27.

Times-Journal photo by Lindsay Slater

OPPOSITE: A girl mourns the loss of a loved one at Town Creek Cemetery in Rainsville. A total of 34 people died after four tornadoes ripped through DeKalb County on April 27.

Times-Journal photo by Melissa Smith

ABOVE: Debris, such as a child's cup, was scattered throughout after DeKalb County's deadliest and most destructive storms in history.

Times-Journal photo by Melissa Smith

BELOW: Tornado damage was evident not only at Plainview School itself, but also at the school's athletic facilities. *Times-Journal photo by Mandi Cooper*

ABOVE: A toddler plays among the many donations at the Sheriff's Department Tornado Relief Center in Rainsville.

Times-Journal photo by Mark Harrison

TOP: Standing on the roof of a home, this photo was taken of the remains of an outbuilding still standing amid the tornado's devastation.

Times-Journal photo by Melissa Smith

BOTTOM: The DeKalb County Schools Coliseum in Rainsville suffered significant damage after being hit by an EF-5 tornado.

Times-Journal photo by Mandi Coope

TOP: Sheet metal from a home lay hanging in a tree with other debris scattered around a home on County Road 27 near Sylvania.

Times-Journal photo by Lonnie McKelvey

BOTTOM: In the days following April 27, many residents in the High Point community near Ider found shelter in tents while keeping their belongings close.

Times-Journal photo by Melissa Smith

FAR RIGHT: Little remained from the devastation of a tornado along this road in the High Point community near Ider.

Times-Journal photo by Melissa Smith

ABOVE: A boat still in tact after the storms stood in front of a hollowed-out shell of a home along with a warning for thieves.

Times-Journal photo by Lindsay Slater

LEFT: Tornado victims gathered what remained of the contents of their homes along County Road 27 near Sylvania in the days following April 27.

Times-Journal photo by Melissa Smith

OPPOSITE: Trees and power poles were snapped by nearly 200 mph winds from an EF-5 tornado that ripped through Rainsville and across DeKalb County on April 27.

Times-Journal photo by Lindsay Slater

GET STORM DEVELOPMENTS AT WWW.TIMESJOURNAL.COM

Times-Journal

DEKALB COUNTY'S OLDEST NEWSPAPER

May 4, 2011

WEDNESDAY

Only 50 cents

Normal Will Eventually Come to DeKalb County ■ *Page 4*

OUR RESOLVE

CURFEWS: Curfews were officially lifted in most of DeKalb, remaining in place in areas still without power.
Page 2

OTHER WORDS: The nation's newspapers show their support for Alabama through their words.
Page 4

RAINSVILLE: The city of Rainsville is considering borrowing money to meet growing costs from the storm.
Page 11

SCHOOLS: All but four DeKalb County schools were back in session this morning after a week out of class.
Page 11

Brother Robby Ferguson (center), pastor at Fuller Baptist Church in also, helps unload supplies Wednesday as the small church continues to provide comfort.

Volunteers prep Wednesday in Rainsville before sorting through truckloads of supplies delivered from Auburn.

THOSE WE LOST

Chelsie Black
Charlotte Bladsworth
Belinda Boatner
Gene Bullock
Marcello Bullock
Jewell Ewing
Emma Ferguson
Jeremy Ferguson
Tonya Ferguson
Kenneth Graham
Linda Graham
Ruth Hairston
Harold Harcrow
Patricia Harcrow
Jody Holvenga
Lethal Lusk
Michael Kilgore
Courtney McGaha
William Michaels
Martha Michaels
Edith Miller
Me Ott
Timothy Ott
Ester Rowan
Peggy Sparks

Roy Durham spent time in biker on Wednesday turning debris left by powerful tornadoes that devastated DeKalb.

Help brings so many to tears

By Mark Harrison

NWS: Tornado number now 3

By Jared Felkins

ABOVE: An ominous sky was evident above the DeKalb County Schools Coliseum just days after a tornado nearly completely destroyed the building in Rainsville.

Photo by Jimmy Durham

LEFT: With roof removed, little remained but the refrigerator and cabinets in the kitchen of a home on County Road 27 near Sylvania.

Times-Journal photo by Melissa Smith

OPPOSITE LEFT TOP: Just days after tornadoes ripped through DeKalb County, Congressman Robert Aderholt (right) toured the damaged areas with Rainsville Mayor Donnie Chandler.

Times-Journal photo by Gloria Jackson

OPPOSITE LEFT BOTTOM: Piles of clothes donated after the April 27 storms filled the DeKalb County Sheriff's Department Relief Center in Rainsville.

Times-Journal photo by Melissa Smith

OPPOSITE RIGHT: One week following devastating tornadoes, the Times-Journal continued its coverage of the destruction that remained, as well as the ongoing recovery.

Times-Journal image

ABOVE: An EF-5 tornado picked up a school bus from the Plainview School parking lot in Rainsville, flattened it and deposited it on the other side of Highway 35.

Photo by Jimmy Durham

LEFT: Members of Mountain View Baptist Church recover the pulpit after an EF-5 tornado destroyed the church April 27.

Times-Journal photo by Melissa Smith

LEFT BOTTOM: Fuller Baptist Church in Ider received donations from the community in the form of diapers and other necessities for children to be given to tornado victims.

Times-Journal photo by Melissa Smith

BELOW: Debris from a destroyed home in the High Point community near Ider collected at the banks of a pond.

Times-Journal photo by Melissa Smith

ABOVE: The American flag flew at Fort Payne City Hall days after April 27.

Times-Journal photo by Lindsay Slater

RIGHT: High winds from a devastating tornado on April 27 knocked out windows at this Ider home.

Times-Journal photo by Melissa Smith

OPPOSITE: Sola in Rainsville was one of the largest industries to be hit by an EF-5 tornado on April 27 as storms ripped through DeKalb County.

Times-Journal photo by Melissa Smith

OUR SURVIVAL

Residents pick up the pieces

Editor's Note: This story originally appeared in the May 5, 2011 edition of the Times-Journal.

APRIL 27 WILL BE BURNED in the minds of so many in DeKalb County for so long.

Residents awakened in the early hours that morning to the sound of tornado sirens that would echo throughout the evening hours.

With power out and weather radios offline, few had any way of knowing what tragedy would come later that night.

Peggy Blevins and four of her family members were huddled together in their small home near Community Credit Union, which was decimated. Neighbors of the Blevins did not make it out of the storm alive.

Through fragile emotions, she described her experience.

"I will never forget that sound," Blevins said, as tears broke through. "The whole house was just vibrating and shaking. Then, the home came down on top of us."

Long-time, family friend Cindy Biddle said there isn't a way to sum up the tragedy.

"It's just devastating," Biddle said. "No words can describe it."

A few houses down from the Blevins, the Bailey's sat with no power, knowing there was a tornado warning, but didn't know where the storm was at or where it was headed.

"The weather siren went off at Plainview," Debra Bailey said. "We had lost power, and I knew there was a warning, but didn't know what area the warning was for."

A few minutes later, Bailey heard the siren again, only it wasn't the siren.

"I thought it was the siren, and I went to look out the front door, and there it was," Bailey said. "I yelled to my husband that it was going to hit us. I had never seen anything like it."

The storm left the Bailey's house with damage to the roof and the surrounding yard.

"When it came through, the house was cracking and popping," Bailey said. "It was terrifying. It shook the house badly."

David Parris, his father and several other family members were in a storm shelter underneath their mobile home. They were sifting through what was left of their belongings on Friday. The storm appeared to have picked the mobile home up with all their possessions inside and dropped it across the road on an embankment. A sea of material possessions like clothing, pictures, and books rested among splintered trees and downed power lines.

"It took the trailer right off the top of us," Parris said. "My dad was holding onto a chain when the door came off of the shelter."

Parris said his father was sucked out of the opening and was pinned underneath a propane gas tank in the front yard.

"That saved him from getting taken further by the storm," Parris said.

Parris said once the home was gone, a retaining wall toppled onto him and his dog.

"When the wall fell, it crushed and killed my dog, who was on top of me," Parris said. "I laid there with him for about 20 minutes before the neighbors helped rescue me."

Through the tragedy, there is the community, which Biddle said she is blessed to be a part of it.

"It's amazing how people have come in," Biddle said. "It doesn't matter if they are you're worst enemy, they'll help you through something like this."

— Lindsay Slater
Staff Writer

OPPOSITE: Residents survey the damage done to a home in Rainsville after it was gutted by a powerful tornado.

Times-Journal photo by Gloria Jackson

ABOVE: Katy's Katfish in Rainsville received significant damage from devastating tornadoes that ripped through DeKalb County.

Times-Journal photo by Mandi Cooper

RIGHT: Displaced family pets were also victims of the deadly tornadoes that moved through DeKalb County on April 27.

Times-Journal photo by Melissa Smith

OPPOSITE: Erick Smith stands in the midst of the destruction brought by April 27 tornadoes that ripped through County Road 27 near Sylvania and other parts of DeKalb County.

Times-Journal photo by Melissa Smith

RIGHT: Anna and Cody Goins mourn the loss of their 3-year-old daughter, Hannah, who died in an April 27 tornado, at a candlelight vigil in Rainsville.

Times-Journal photo by Lindsay Slater

BELOW: This framed drawing depicting Jesus was surrounded by broken glass but remained in tact at a Sylvania home.

Times-Journal photo by Melissa Smith

ABOVE: Hope arose from the pulpit of Mountain View Baptist Church where Carpenters for Christ traveled from South Alabama to help rebuild it.

Times-Journal photo by Melissa Smith

LEFT: An American flag lay hanging on a tree stump amid the destruction found on County Road 27 near Sylvania.

Times-Journal photo by Melissa Smith

RIGHT: A Times-Journal newspaper box remained untouched in the center of a demolished Huddle House in Rainsville.

Times-Journal photo by Mandi Cooper

OPPOSITE: Only the shell of a brick home remained in Rainsville immediately after tornadoes ripped through DeKalb County on April 27.

Times-Journal photo by Melissa Smith

BELOW: More than a week after April 27 brought devastation and destruction, the Times-Journal continued to publish important information for victims, volunteers and readers.

Times-Journal image

GET STORM DEVELOPMENTS AT WWW.TIMES-JOURNAL.COM

DEKALB COUNTY'S OLDEST NEWSPAPER

TIMES-JOURNAL
THURSDAY
May 5, 2011   Only 50 cents

Photographer Tells Harrowing Tale of Tornado ▪ Page 4

OUR SURVIVAL

SCHOOLS LEFT WITH DECISIONS: DeKalb officials continue to make plans for students.
Page 2

POWER CLOSER TO BEING RESTORED: By Wednesday county was expected to be back online.
Page 9

RECOVERY ONGOING THANKS TO MANY: Help continues to flood to DeKalb from outside areas.
Page 3

MUCH MORE NEEDED FOR RECOVERY: Items are still wanted to help with the tornado response.
Page 10

Residents continue to sift through rubble where homes once stood in Rainsville. Families survived three deadly tornadoes that roared through DeKalb on April 27.

Tragedy still

Helping You Help
The Relief Effort

LEFT: Alan Smith, owner of Williams Service Station in the High Point community near Ider, offers a meal to a tornado victim.

Times-Journal photo by Melissa Smith

OPPOSITE: Many homes in the path of destruction through DeKalb County remained with significant damage and missing roofs as debris lay all around.

Times-Journal photo by Mark Harrison

BELOW: Ronald McCurdy points to the path of devastation left by April 27 tornadoes on his ATV in the High Point community.

Times-Journal photo by Melissa Smith

ABOVE: Ranee Roberts, a Williams Service Station employee, shows what remained of the room in the back of the station where she survived a tornado's near direct hit.

Times-Journal photo by Melissa Smith

LEFT: Betty Smith looks into the storm shelter where she rode out the deadly tornadoes April 27 in the High Point community near Ider.

Times-Journal photo by Melissa Smith

BELOW: A large number of headstones and other cement markers remained tattered but in tact at Town Creek Cemetery in Rainsville.

Times-Journal photo by Melissa Smith

TOP: A woman shows the closet that provided shelter for her, her husband and three children on County Road 27 near Sylvania.

Times-Journal photo by Melissa Smith

BOTTOM: Damage and destruction lay just outside the door at the Hester home in Ider, which was partially destroyed by a tornado.

Times-Journal photo by Melissa Smith

FAR LEFT: A camper trailer was placed near where a home used to stand in Ider. The path of devastation from April 27 tornadoes was ¾-mile wide in some areas.

Times-Journal photo by Melissa Smith

ABOVE: Fuller Baptist Church in Ider served as a distribution center for food and other supplies for tornado victims.

Times-Journal photo by Melissa Smith

RIGHT TOP: The trunk of a large oak tree remained splintered after tornadoes ripped through the Lakeview community.

Times-Journal photo by Diane Sanders

RIGHT BOTTOM: Pets, such as this dachshund, were picked up and taken to the DeKalb County Animal Adoption Center in Fort Payne until they could be reunited with their owners.

Times-Journal photo by Melissa Smith

OPPOSITE: An aerial view of Rainsville shows the destruction after a tornado ripped through the Sola building.

Times-Journal photo by Melissa Smith

ABOVE: A view of the cheap seats in the DeKalb County Schools Coliseum was visible after an EF-5 tornado removed the outer walls of the building.

Times-Journal photo by Jared Felkins

RIGHT: In between tornado episodes April 27, Sand Mountain Electric Cooperative workers assess damaged power lines near Powell.

Times-Journal photo by Melissa Smith

LEFT: Following DeKalb County's deadliest storms, hundreds gathered in Rainsville for a candlelight vigil to mourn the loss of loved ones.

Times-Journal photo by Lindsay Slater

OUR STRENGTH

Structure in ruins; Mountain View survives

Editor's Note: This story originally appeared in the May 3, 2011 edition of the Times-Journal.

THE ORIGINAL BUILDING FOR MOUNTAIN View Baptist Church in Sylvania was constructed in 1902.

It had stood through 19 presidencies, two world wars, the Great Depression, the moon shot and 9/11. It had seen more than a century of sunrises and sunsets.

Until Wednesday. Battered, beaten and torn apart, the old church was transformed into a pile of rubble by severe storms, including an EF-5 tornado.

The congregation held services on the church grounds Sunday morning, with many bringing lawn chairs and the Rev. Brian Harris speaking from a makeshift pulpit.

Glorandle Graham, 68 and a member for 56 years, got a close look at the destruction when she sat up front for the service.

"It's beyond me," she said of what happened to the church her ancestors helped build.

But what wasn't destroyed was the spirit of the people who worship at Mountain View. They were joined for part of the service by Gov. Robert Bentley, who was touring damaged areas in Sylvania and Rainsville.

"It was good to have the governor here to show us that he cares about us and that he's a fellow Christian," said Greg Graham, Glorandle's son and a church deacon.

Harris echoed those thoughts.

"In times like these it helps to see that our government cares for us. We're thankful that he was here," he said.

Sylvania Mayor Mitch Dendy was also in attendance.

"I think it's the most impressive thing that I've seen in my 49 years of life — politicians coming together to worship the Lord," he said. "I think it shows that he cares so much about helping that he's going to do a good job. I believe he's a people person. That shows a man's character."

Dendy said he met with Bentley's cabinet prior to the service.

"They said the governor wanted to know if we were getting everything we had asked for. If we weren't he wanted to make it happen," Dendy said.

As the town begins to recover and rebuild, the church plans to do the same. Harris said Mountain View would turn the destruction into a ministry. He said the focus would not be reconstructing buildings, but rather, helping people rebuild lives.

"I'm thankful that there was nobody here," Harris said looking back on Wednesday's events. "We had called off services that night and didn't lose any of our church members."

In the pile of rubble where the original building once stood, a white quilt was visible Sunday. It was retrieved by a church member following the service.

Dirty but intact, it was symbolic of the congregation's resiliency. It, like them, was a storm survivor.

— Lew Gilliland
Sports Editor

OPPOSITE: Gov. Robert Bentley and his wife, Dianne, pray for lives lost on April 27 at a church gathering at Mountain View Baptist Church on May 1.

Photo by Mary Felkins

ABOVE: The fence surrounding Plainview School baseball field was one of several examples of damage to the school and athletic facilities.

Times-Journal photo by Melissa Smith

RIGHT: Betty Smith finds a framed picture of her in-laws among the debris at her home in the High Point community near Ider.

Times-Journal photo by Melissa Smith

OPPOSITE: Kay and Alan Smith share a hug amid the remains of Williams Service Station in the High Point community near Ider.

Times-Journal photo by Melissa Smith

ABOVE: Emotions ran high May 1 during services at the remains of Pine Grove Methodist Church in the High Point community.

Times-Journal photo by Melissa Smith

RIGHT: DeRinda Blevins collects items from the remains of her home on Marshall Road in Rainsville.

Times-Journal photo by Lindsay Slater

OPPOSITE LEFT: Lisa Shaddix sifts through the remains of a home on County Road 27 near Sylvania days after tornadoes destroyed it.

Times-Journal photo by Melissa Smith

OPPOSITE RIGHT: Jonah Martin and others share an emotional moment following the April 27 storms at Martin's home on County Road 27.

Times-Journal photo by Melissa Smith

ABOVE: Plainview High School students gathered at a candlelight vigil in Rainsville to mourn the loss of classmate, Courtney McGaha, and others who were killed April 27.

Times-Journal photo by Lindsay Slater

LEFT: Country music supergroup Alabama members Teddy Gentry (left) and Randy Owen announce the Bama Rising benefit concert in Birmingham that raised millions for tornado relief. *Times-Journal photo by Mark Harrison*

LEFT: Mountain View Baptist Church members gather at a makeshift altar May 1 during the church's first service since a tornado destroyed the building.

Photo by Mary Felkins

BELOW: A High Point community resident shows workers the path of destruction from deadly tornadoes at his home.

Times-Journal photo by Melissa Smith

ABOVE: Volunteers cooked and served meals at the Rainsville Fire Hall for both tornado victims and fellow volunteers.

Times-Journal photo by Gloria Jackson

RIGHT: Bricks, trees and other debris lay piled around Mountain View Baptist Church as the building was destroyed April 27 by an EF-5 tornado.

Times-Journal photo by Melissa Smith

TOP: A wall at this home was detached from the others as sunlight shown in after a tornado did significant damage there April 27.

Times-Journal photo by Melissa Smith

BOTTOM: Little remained of this home in Rainsville after taking a near-direct hit from an EF-5 tornado that ripped through DeKalb County.

Times-Journal photo by Lindsay Slater

TOP: Tents and campers became makeshift homes for many on County Road 140 in Ider and across Sand Mountain in the days after tornadoes ripped through DeKalb on April 27.

Times-Journal photo by Melissa Smith

RIGHT: The devastating path of a tornado can be seen on this ridge as trees were blown over by high winds from the storm.

Times-Journal photo by Melissa Smith

FAR RIGHT: Thousands of power lines, poles and towers were toppled by April 27 tornadoes, leaving many without power for about a week or longer.

Times-Journal photo by Melissa Smith

ABOVE: Fuel became sparce in the days following April 27. Bruce's Foodland Plus Fuel Center found itself with long lines from those waiting to fill their tanks.

Times-Journal photo by Lindsay Slater

DEKALB COUNTY'S OLDEST NEWSPAPER

Times-Journal

FRIDAY

May 6, 2011

Only 50 cents

BACK TO THE BEGINNING: Left in ruins, Grace Baptist Church will rise from destruction.
Page 7

TORNADO NUMBER GROWING: NWS officials continue to learn more about storms.
Page 3

OUR STRENGTH

Volunteers stop at noon to pray Thursday at the DeKalb County Sheriff's Department relief distribution center in Rainsville in honor of National Day of Prayer.
Times-Journal photo by Melissa Smith

Prayer power hits DeKalb

By Lindsay Slater
lslater@times-journal.com

Never underestimate the power of prayer.

The DeKalb County Sheriff's Department Distribution Center in Rainsville was abuzz Thursday with people loading cars and unloading trucks full of supplies. Citizens affected by the tornadoes were going through items to find things they needed.

Everyone stopped at noon for about 15 minutes to recognize the National Day of Prayer, which is held on the first Thursday of May each year.

This year marks the 60th anniversary of the annual observance.

■ See **Prayer, 3**

Photo by Melissa Smith
Tears and hope come to volunteers who pray Thursday.

MORE COVERAGE
POWER UPDATE: Sand Mountain Electric turns lights on for about 5,000 customers Wednesday night.
Page 8

◯ PHOTO GALLERIES
Get a complete visual timeline of DeKalb's response

Schools get help for missed days

By Mark Harrison
mharrison@times-journal.com

It's unlikely Fort Payne City or DeKalb County students will have to make up days of school missed since tornadoes ripped through April 27 thanks to a state law signed by Gov. Robert Bentley on Thursday.

"I'm already filling out paperwork to ask for a waiver for the days missed," said DeKalb County superintendent Charles Warren.

DeKalb County students missed five days in most schools due to tornadoes, but Plainview, Henagar, Ider and Sylvania remain out and are expected to return to classes Monday.

Although no Fort Payne schools suffered damage during the storms that decimated portions of DeKalb County on April 27, the schools were closed for two days due to power outages.

■ See **Schools, 3**

ABOVE: Robby Ferguson and others load supplies for tornado victims at Fuller Baptist Church in Ider.

Times-Journal photo by Melissa Smith

LEFT: After more than a week following April 27, the Times-Journal continued its coverage of the effects of deadly tornadoes as relief turned into recovery.

Times-Journal image

OPPOSITE: Volunteers and workers joined tornado victims in a moment of prayer during the National Day of Prayer at the DeKalb Sheriff's Department Relief Center.

Times-Journal photo by Mark Harrison

ABOVE: It's sometimes the little things found that make the difference, such as a pocket knife found by an Ider man.

Times-Journal photo by Melissa Smith

RIGHT: Prayer became the norm among volunteers and tornado victims at the Sheriff's Department Relief Center in Rainsville.

Times-Journal photo by Melissa Smith

OPPOSITE: Stamp Baptist Church in Ider was one of several churches in DeKalb County either partially or completely destroyed by April 27 tornadoes.

Times-Journal photo by Melissa Smith

OUR FUTURE

From April's destruction will come new DeKalb

Editor's Note: This column originally appeared in the May 4, 2011 edition of the Times-Journal.

CHILDHOOD WAS FILLED WITH SKINNED knees, playing under the dining room table and not understanding things grandma used to say.

Right in the middle of relocating the Times-Journal's mobile newsroom for the fourth time, there was a calm that seemed unnatural. After three solid days of answering calls, texts and posting information at times-journal.com around the clock, it was then when I took a deep breath.

The sun was shining and sky blue and beautiful far away from the damage and destruction of two EF-4 tornadoes that decimated much of DeKalb County. It was Sunday.

As the mind wandered, it went back to a more simple time playing around grandmother's house. Tornadoes were still a concern, newspapers were around – they were there for sports scores, honor rolls and the occasional class picture – but the Internet was a place where you put fish when one got on the line.

It was then when one of my grandmother's old sayings popped into the old noggin. She used to say, "April showers bring May flowers."

Just think about that for a minute. Let it roll off the tongue a few times. How fitting was that simple cliché in the grand scheme of things Sunday.

Sunday separated four days from hundreds of thousands of people affected by some of the most devastating storms DeKalb County and all of Alabama has ever seen. It provided distance from the lack of power, the destruction, the relief efforts, the shelters filled with people who lost everything and the deaths of friends and loved ones.

THAT WAS APRIL; THIS IS MAY

It never struck me how much incredible power that simple phrase my grandmother used to say when, at that moment, the past and present became the future. April turned into May.

It would be difficult for anyone to say they haven't mourned, cried, sobbed and were generally saddened in the wake of so much destruction. That's the past, and we should never forget.

As recovery begins, so does cleaning, picking up the pieces and making what was once old, new again. That's the present, and we should all pitch in to do what we can.

As eyes looked to the sky Sunday, however, the future began. It's time to look there, after all.

There's no fault in living in all three.

The future holds bright things for DeKalb County. It means new houses, farms, buildings, and things. It means making new memories and gathering new hope.

So while my grandmother's old saying brought just a glimmer of comfort to a world turned upside down, maybe it's time for a new one.

Maybe it's time, now, to say "April destruction brings May hope."

After all, it's May now.

— Jared Felkins
Managing Editor

OPPOSITE: Kira Ferguson, 2, sits on a table at Fuller Baptist Church in Ider as volunters work to prepare food for tornado victims.

Times Journal photo by Melissa Smith

ABOVE: A resident in Ider works to repair his roof after it was severely damaged by April 27 tornadoes.

Times-Journal phot by Mark Harrison

RIGHT: Jonah Martin says a prayer at the base of a cross he built in his front yard after tornadoes ripped through DeKalb County on April 27.

Times-Journal photo by Melissa Smith

OPPOSITE: William Smith and Don Hoskins, both of Sylvania, work to repair damage caused by an EF-5 tornado April 27 at Wayne Young's farm on Sylvania Gap Road.

Times-Journal photo by Mark Harrison

RIGHT: Steven Caneer plays with his dog, Stormy, at Williams Service Station in the High Point community near Ider.

Times-Journal photo by Melissa Smith

OPPOSITE LEFT: Volunteers with Carpenters for Christ help to rebuild Mountain View Baptist Church in Sylvania.

Times-Journal photo by Melissa Smith

OPPOSITE RIGHT TOP: A Sylvania boy sifts through debris at his home on County Road 27 near Sylvania after an EF-4 tornado destroyed it on April 27.

Times-Journal photo by Melissa Smith

OPPOSITE RIGHT BOTTOM: Looking through what remained, this Sylvania girl uncovers items amid the debris that remained from her demolished home on Sylvania Gap Road.

Times-Journal photo by Melissa Smith

ABOVE: Roy Durham spent time in Ider burning debris left by powerful tornadoes that devastated DeKalb County.

Times-Journal photo by Melissa Smith

LEFT: Wills Valley Elementary School's Dimes for Disaster effort netted more than $9,000 for DeKalb disaster relief. Students were asked to collect dimes for tornado victims. Pictured (from front) are students Kenzie Akins, Meg Martin, Ella Fowler, Abby Boatwright and Cooper Perea collecting the dimes donated.

Times-Journal photo by Jared Felkins

OPPOSITE: A volunteeer cuts limbs from downed trees caused by devastating tornadoes that ripped through DeKalb County on April 27.

Times-Journal photo by Melissa Smith

ABOVE: Mountain View Baptist Church members and pastor Brian Harris (far right) go over plans to rebuild the church after it was destroyed.

Times-Journal photo by Mark Harrison

LEFT: Paydence Smalley enjoys a snack at the Ider Rescue Squad building.

Times-Journal photo by Melissa Smith

OPPOSITE: Contract workers with the U.S. Army Corps of Engineers work to clean up debris along the right of way of County Road 27.

Times-Journal photo by Melissa Smith

ABOVE: After days became weeks following devastating tornadoes ripped through DeKalb County on April 27, signs of gratitude could be found.

Times-Journal photo by Melissa Smith

RIGHT: Flames at a candlelight vigil shown bright in memory of loved ones lost in the deadliest storm in DeKalb County history.

Times-Journal photo by Lindsay Slater

THE TIME WILL COME WHEN WE ARE NEEDED

Editor's Note: This column originally appeared in the May 7-8, 2011 edition of the Times-Journal.

THERE WILL BE A DAY when we are needed again. There will be a time when someone's desperation will rival our own. Disaster will indeed return.

It will rise along the banks of the Mississippi. It will roar along our precious Gulf Coast. It will blow along the Atlantic coast, roll across the plains and shake California. There will be hurricanes and tornadoes and great snowstorms and earthquakes and tsunamis.

They will destroy homes and businesses and churches and families and towns and lives. In their wake, they will leave heartache, confusion and painful deaths. They will swipe hope from places that never seemed to be without it.

Disasters will return. They always do.

That's when we will be needed again.

That's when we will again feel our pain and rejoice in the comfort that came from that man for New York who brought with him a chainsaw. Or, we will remember the youth group from that little church in northwest Arkansas that dirtied their little fingers to sell plants to raise money for us.

We will smile when we think of the comfort that came from that big, red cross and the hearts from Florida and Ohio and Iowa and Indiana and Massachusetts that came along with it.

Our darkest hours will come flooding back, only to be brightened by the memories of the Amish group from Kentucky who became our friends or the more than two dozen Wisconsin firefighters who came running without the smallest idea where Rainsville or Sylvania or Ider or Henagar or Flat Rock or Higdon was.

We live now with the absolute knowledge of love and kindness and caring. We are the examples of prayer and faith. Prayer has lifted us. Faith has sustained us. The overwhelming generosity of fellow human beings has altered us.

On April 27, the worst natural disaster in our history impacted us. Killer tornadoes, with no care for life or property, cut a path through our community and our hearts. Nature showed its vengeance, its fury and its unimaginable power.

It frightened us. It left us in tears. It affected us. But, it did not change us. Those who came running with open arms and warm hearts did that. They changed us for the better. Tornadoes left behind rubble and worry. Those who rushed to us will leave behind a complete confidence in the affect one life can have on another.

One day, we will be needed again. The call may come from thousands of miles away or it could be from down the street. But, we will be needed. That will be our time to change lives, and there is no question the people of this community will accept that challenge.

— J.D. Davidson
President and Publisher

RIGHT: Harold Dean Mitchell led the congregation at Pine Grove United Methodist Church in songs during services where the church once stood before April 27 tornadoes.

Times-Journal photo by Mark Harrison

On April 27, just a few minutes of darkness cast a spotlight on pillars of strength and compassion.

Our Community. Our Hospital.

It wasn't the tornado on April 27 that defined us as a community, but rather our response in the minutes, hours, days and weeks that followed. At DeKalb Regional Medical Center, we couldn't be more proud of our community and its compassion, resiliency and steadfastness in the face of such tremendous difficulties. As your community hospital, our pledge to you is that we will always be there to offer a helping hand – in both good times and bad – to those we have the good fortune of calling our neighbors, friends and family.

DEKALB REGIONAL
MEDICAL CENTER

www.DeKalbRegional.com

Medical personnel rush to aid injured

By Mark Harrison
mharrison@times-journal.com

Those old enough to remember the television show M.A.S.H., or the movie that preceded it, might have an idea of what it was like in DeKalb County Regional Medical Center emergency room April 27.

So too, might those who have actually previously experienced war and disaster firsthand, according to Fort Payne pediatrician Dr. David Atchley.

"It was organized chaos," he said. "Patients were coming in by waves."

M.A.S.H., of course, stands for Mobile Army Surgical Hospital –

us in a position to be able to respond accordingly."

Rains said 93 victims were treated in the hospital's ER on the day of the storm itself and, during the seven days that followed, treated a total of 211 patients who suffered injuries related to the storms.

"The thing I'm most proud of is that of those 211 patients, especially the 93 we saw that first evening, we did not have a single patient who passed away while under our care," Rains said. "That speaks volumes about the level of dedication to care and compassion that our doctors, nurses and support personnel have for the community."

That included DeKalb Ambulance Service setting up a triage center at Rainsville Fire Department to take care of those with less critical injuries.

"Hands down, it's the worst disaster we've ever had to deal with," said Mark Ford, DAS director.

He said the ambulance service, with help from ambulances from Albertville firefighters and A-Med out of Marshall County, 40 patients injured in the storm were taken to the fire department and some 80 patents were taken to various trauma care hospitals outside the area.

"What we did last week, we just

"We were flooded with patients."

Michelle Mays
15-year veteran emergency room nurse at DeKalb Regional Medical Center

LIFE CHANGING

All personnel respond at DeKalb Regional

By Mark Harrison
mharrison@times-journal.com

Michelle Mays has been an emergency room nurse for 15 years. In that time, she's seen plenty, but never anything like the scenes that unfolded after the tornadoes that devas-

injured wasn't enough for Mays. Only a few days later, she was on the ground at her church, Breakthrough Church of God in Sylvania, helping to feed the hungry.

Jennifer Mays, wife of church pastor David Mays, said the feeding efforts were an extension

Mays said she's never experienced so intense a situation, but said personnel at DRMC pulled together to handle the crisis.

"All our doctor's came in," she said. " We had people coming to help from all over the hospital,

Last Sunday afternoon, the church – like so many other churches in the area – did just that, grilling food and feeding more than 200 in the afternoon.

Just down the road in Rainsville, another area hit heavily by the storm, Boyd Scott said he feels blessed to still be alive. The storm knocked out

---

ding th

ls and hambu

Slater
al.com

t and
e lives
d
knew is

remain
the
ing
ise of
w,
teers
en

DeKalb County Sheriff's Office

In all my years of law enforcement I have never witnessed such devastation as DeKalb County suffered from the tornadoes of April 27, 2011. We have mourned those lost, prayed for the injured, and provided assistance to those with property destroyed. I have never been more proud of our community, and it is our prayer that this spirit of service will continue as we face long-term recovery. We believe that with hard work and prayers, our community can emerge and rebuild even stronger than it was before.

Jimmy Harris

Jimmy Harris
Sheriff, DeKalb County

"For I was hungry and you gave me food, I was thirsty and you gave me drink, I was a stranger and you welcomed me, I was naked and you clothed me."
Matthew 25:35-36

DeKalb County

MAY NEVER BE THE SAME

IT WILL BE STRONGER.

DeKalb County Commission

This tornado photo courtesy of Jimmy Durham

Ricky Harcrow
President

Jerome Tinker
District 1

Ed Nix
District 2

Chris Kuykendall
District 3

DeWitt Jackson
District 4

111 Grand Avenue SW • Suite 200 • Fort Payne, AL 35967 • (256) 845-8500 • www.dekalbcountyal.us

In Remembrance

In memory of the lives lost as a result of the devastating tornadoes which struck DeKalb County on April 27, 2011.

TIMES-JOURNAL
Fort Payne, Alabama

Chelsea Black, 20, Higdon

Charlotte Bludsworth, 36, Rainsville

Belinda Sue Boatner, 67, Higdon

Eddie Joe Bobbitt, 71, Rainsville

Gene Bullock, 65, Rainsville

Marcella Bullock, 64, Rainsville

Jewell Tinker Ewing, 73, Higdon

Emma Ferguson, 6, Sylvania

Jeremy Ferguson, 34, Sylvania

Tawnya Ferguson, 33, Sylvania

Hannah Goins, 3, Rainsville

Kenneth Graham, 56, Valley Head

Linda Martin Graham, 61, Valley Head

Violet Ruth Hairston, 90, Fort Payne

Harold Harcrow, 74, Rainsville

Patricia Harcrow, 75, Rainsville

Jody Huizenga, 28, Fort Payne

Lethel Izell, 86, Rainsville

Jimmy Michael Kilgore, 48, Sylvania

Courtney McGaha, 15, Fort Payne

Martha Michaels, 72, Higdon

William "Buddy" Michaels, 70, Higdon

Eula Miller, 80, Fyffe

Ida Ott, 87, Henagar

Timothy Ott, 53, Henagar

Esther Rosson, 81, Rainsville

Peggy Lwanda Sparks, 55, Rainsville

Terry Tubb Tinker, 50, Higdon

Jidal Vermillion, 44, Fort Payne

William Daniel Vermillion, 42, Fort Payne

Arnold Wayne White, 68, Ider

Judith Austin White, 63, Ider

Hubert Wooten, 70, Rainsville

Juanita Wooten, 70, Rainsville